SPILLED WORDS

THE CRIMSON KISS QUOTE COLLECTION

Cici. B

Dedicated to all of the women who feel like they're alone in their feelings...

because it helps to know that you're not.

This letter, is for you...

Before you get into the Quote Collection, I just wanted to seriously thank each and every one of you for rocking with me the way you do. The way you all have shown me love, has been *incredible*, and while so many of you write to me every day to tell me that I've helped you through your struggles, and have inspired you to be better through my stories, I don't think you know just how much you all have inspired me to keep going in return.

See, I took a chance on myself when I first started sharing my writings for the world to read, and it wasn't easy. There was nothing flowery, or politically correct about my words. I wasn't the writer who wrote a bunch of clean, pretty poems with perfect grammar that floated on sugarcoated clouds after the sun set to sound nice...

I was the complete opposite.

I didn't give a fuck about "sounding nice". I gave a fuck about telling my stories exactly the way I lived, and felt them.

● ● ●

I know that I caught many people off guard in the beginning. For the first 4-5 months of my "social media debut" every day, there would always be at least one person in my comments, under my posts, complaining about my choice of words. Telling me that it's not "lady like" to swear the way that I do. Appalled that I was so blunt and open about my experiences with men, and taken aback at how many times I was pointing a blame finger towards myself, rather than at men in general.

I remember at one point, someone rather close to me suggested that maybe I should dial back on both the swearing, and the raw vulnerability in my work. They said that I was hurting my own growth on social media, and that most people prefer things that sound softer, and feel lighter.

I don't think they quite understood what they were actually suggesting I should do, by saying that to me—in a nutshell, they were suggesting that I be someone that I'm not. They were suggesting that I change who I am, and dilute the ink in my pen, to appease the masses, as opposed to touching those who feel and think like I do.

I'm so tired of people like that. I'm so tired of people constantly trying to fit everyone into the "perfect" box: the box that is easier on the eyes, the box with the pretty ribbons, the box with classy glitter.
Not everyone is made for those boxes. And not everyone needs to be in them.

I'm not stupid. I am well aware that if I were to write just a little cleaner, a little safer, and more "general," I'd have triple the following that I do now. I know that if I were to write "how to" guides, like for example "how to get over your narcissistic ex boyfriend" or "how to learn to love yourself better"—I'd be selling books out the crack of my ass. But I'd also be selling myself out—because that is not what I'm about, that is not what lives inside of me, and that is not who I am.

I stood my ground, and fought to be myself through my writing, and eventually people realized that I wasn't fucking changing, or selling myself out for no one. Eventually, all of the wrong people left, and all of

the right people came, and stayed.
The right people, being all of you.
I'm proud of myself for not
succumbing to people's opinions of
who I should be to please *them*, and
furthermore, I'm elated that my
readers are women who adore my
rawness, and who wouldn't want it
any other way.

See, a reader's responsibility is not
to tell authors how, or what to write.
A reader's responsibility, is to
understand that everything isn't for
everyone, and to then find the
authors that are already writing
about what they love, what they
need, what they want to get lost in,
what they feel or want to feel, and/or
what they relate to.
In turn, an author's responsibility is
to stay true to themselves, and to
be/create their own waves, rather
than follow other people's.

No matter what we do in this world,
there will always be people who love
us for it, and there will always be
those who can't stand us for it.
What's important, is that we get to a
point where we love ourselves, and
what we're doing, so much...
that we're all the way cool with both
sides of the spectrum.

So again, thank you from the middle of my heart, to all of you who have supported, and understood me, and who have respected my individuality, creativity, heart, soul, and mind, and have rocked heavily with it all. I am forever grateful.

Without even realizing it, you all had a hand in teaching me how to be more and more comfortable with being myself, and now that you know that, I hope that this inspires you to be more and more comfortable with being yourselves too.

Much, much love...

your girl,

B.

SPILLED WORDS

The Fucking Nerve.

So he found you—the perfect woman for him.

You're the type of woman he's always dreamed of settling down, and building a life with. There was just one problem. He stumbled onto you too soon. He wasn't ready for you yet. He still wanted to do the single guy shit and live only for himself—and there's nothing wrong with that. I mean, there wouldn't have been anything wrong with that, had he been honest about it. Right? But what did he do instead? He lied. Told you he *was* ready. Asked for your heart and held it hostage by giving you a relationship to your face, but continuing to be the single guy behind your back.

Awesome.

So now, here you are... fighting and arguing with him because you want back what's fucking yours—you want your heart back. And there he is... staring directly at the pain gushing out through

* * *

your eyes, as your screams of anger, embarrassment, and betrayal, pierce the air around him.

And though he knows that he's responsible for this shit, and that you have every right to feel how you feel as a result of this shit... he has the fucking nerve to stand there, and call you...
crazy.

This, is the fucking hard part...

<u>Regretful Moments.</u>

My mistake?

Not listening to that little voice inside of me screaming, *"he's not even fucking worth it."*

Tacenda.

"You confuse me." I wrote in the text. "You confuse me, and I don't like it. Some days you make me feel so alive, but then other days, it's like you're cool with me holding my breath. I don't want to talk to my friends about us, because they aren't in this with us and they don't know you like I know you, but lately even I don't feel like I know you, and so… where are you? Where are we? What are we doing?
Please… say something." I felt a couple of tears sting my cheeks as I finished the text, and right before I hit 'send'...

I decided to delete the entire fucking thing.

Not Today.

"You've just gotta wish him all the best, and keep it moving," said my level-headed friend, and I frowned. "No, fuck. I'm not wishing him all the fucking best—that's just something people say to sound nice, and I don't care about 'sounding' fucking nice when I feel like I wanna throw up every time someone mentions his stupid ass name."

I took a sip of my drink and felt her staring at me. "Don't look at me like that," I told her, and she laughed, making me laugh a little bit too. "It's all good girl," she said. "You're just not there yet, and that's okay. You'll get there eventually."

I stopped the waiter as he was walking by, and ordered us two more drinks. "Yea… eventually. Just not today man. Just not fucking today."

<u>Robbery.</u>

I just remember feeling like I wanted
to take everything back from him—
my touches, my kisses, my sex, my
love, my emotions, my loyalty, my
time, my energy, my conversations,
my compromises, my efforts, my
vulnerability… myself. I absolutely
hated feeling like he was walking
around happily on a daily basis with
all of me, while I was walking around
disturbingly empty, and in that
moment I just wanted to take
everything that had given to him,
fucking back…

that's all.

As Real As It Gets.

Reminding yourself over and over
again that if he wanted to he just
would, while at the same time,
clutching your heart and feeling like
shit because it's crystal clear that he
doesn't want to... and then you can't
even help but ask yourself, but why?
Why doesn't he want to? Why
doesn't he want me the same way
that I want him? Is there something
wrong with me? What is it? Did I do
something wrong? What was it?
How did I get here, and how do I get
the hell out of here? Because fuck...

does this shit ever hurt.

To Teach, Or Not To Teach.

I'm somewhere in-between not wanting to be spiteful—because that's not who I am—but also feeling like maybe it's not about spite. Maybe it's just a matter of you needing to learn your lesson once and for all, and maybe I'm just the woman who is supposed to teach it to you.

This Fucking Heart Of Mine.

"But, so why is it that I still can't bring myself to do anything to hurt his heart, or to disrespect him, even after the way that he's hurt mine and disrespected me?" I asked my girl through a cracking voice as I desperately tried to fight back my tears. "Huh? Tell me. Tell me why, no matter how upset I am, deep down inside, I still don't ever want him to feel the way I feel right now?" She dug into her purse, pulled out a tissue and handed it to me at the exact same moment that my tears won the battle.

"Because," she said, "That just isn't who you are. You're not the type of person who purposely, and spitefully hurts the people you love. Your heart works well girl, and that's a good thing. I know it probably doesn't feel like it right now, but trust me… it's a really good thing that your heart works well."

<u>White Flags.</u>

We'd spend three weeks in love, and
then two weeks in resentment—
throwing it back and forth like a
basketball. One week it was in my
court, the next week it was in his,
and I can't tell you just how many
nights I'd stay up trying to retrace
our steps... trying to figure out how
we let things get this far and out of
control. And on those nights, I would
wonder if he ever did the same. On
those nights, I would wonder if we'd
ever get to a point where we'd finally
raise our white flags, but together,
and at the same time.

<u>Rebel With A Cause.</u>

I'm an easy-going type of girl,

as long as we're going.

You can't try to keep me in a box

And expect me not to eventually

scream, and fight

to break free.

<u>Done It All.</u>

"Okay, so fucking great!" I yelled at him, enraged and exhausted from our never ending emotional roller coaster. "You love me, and I love you—we've said those words a thousand times, it's nothing new. But now what? What are *you* going to do about it? Because I've done all that I could do already!" He pulled me close to him, and held me in his arms as I broke down in tears, beating my fists against his chest. "I've done all that I could do." I said again.

<u>Liquid Danger.</u>

I had locked myself in my house
since our break-up the month
before. I hadn't initiated any contact
with him at all, nor had I responded
to any of the attempts he made to
contact me. My girls—who were over
my depression—decided it was time
to drag me out for a girls night.
By 2AM, I had downed 4 too many
glasses of Cognac, and my very
responsible friends had taken my car
keys away from me… but they
should have taken my phone
instead. I sent him a text, "I fucking
hate you." Almost immediately he
responded "Do you want to see
me?" And I wrote back… "Yes."

Midnight Fucking Madness.

... and I know.

I know that I had no business letting
him back in.
I don't need you to tell me that.

But he was familiar, and he knew
me. He knew what I liked, what I
loved, and what I needed.
There was also no doubt in my mind
that when the morning came, I'd
open my eyes, see him laying there
naked in my bed beside me, and I'd
be fucking furious with myself—for
those next couple of hours though, I
just needed to be touched,
caressed, and held in silence...

by someone who already knew me.

<u>Relapse.</u>

I was slowly getting over him, or so I thought.

But now it felt like I was right back to the day that I walked away from him—a fucking mess.

I shook my head, took a deep breath, wiped the tears off of my face with the back of my hand, and told myself to pull it together and stop crying.

These things happen.

It's not the end of the world.

I'm not the first, and I won't be the last woman on earth…

to relapse.

<u>Dear Diary.</u>

I just don't understand what I did wrong. I stood by his side, and supported him through all of his shit—no matter how heavy it felt on me, or how trying it got for me—I stuck it out.

Love is patient, love is kind… right?

I nurtured him, and built him up— selflessly, and with pleasure— because that's what I was supposed to do as his woman… right? I'm supposed to be his rib, I'm supposed to take care of my king.

But the minute he felt like he was at his strongest… the minute he felt like his broken wings were mended, and ready for flight—it was fuck me. Fuck what I had to say anymore. Fuck how I was feeling. Fuck what I needed from him. Fuck what I deserved… because he was strong now. Stronger than me, because I gave him all of my strength and energy. And I guess I just don't understand how he could use it all, then fly away, happily, and leave me with nothing.

What did I do wrong? Am I not
supposed to love the way that I do?

M.B.F.F

It was probably around 4:30AM
when I called, waking her out of her
sleep. I was crying so hard that I
could barely fucking talk. You know
the type of crying that you do when
you're hurting badly, but on the
inside? Yeah… it was that kind. All I
could manage to tell her was "I need
you right now."
She didn't ask me why. She didn't
even ask what had happened. The
only thing she did ask for, was my
location, and in less than 20 minutes
she walked through my front door in
her pajamas, and a headscarf
wrapped around her hair.
You know who she was?

My best fucking friend.

<u>20/20 Vision.</u>

I remember not being able to look at my friend in the face while I spoke, so I kept my eyes lowered to the ground. See, not only was my heart troubled, but I was also embarrassed that I kept coming to her with the same damn issue over and over again.
I remember the way that she took my hand and squeezed it softly—letting me know she was still on my side—and interrupted me mid-sentence. "Girl, look at me." She said. "Look at me, and listen to me carefully." Slowly, I lifted my head and met her eyes with mine. "You have to stop seeing this man for who you want him to be, and start seeing him for exactly who he is… and who he is…

just isn't good for you."

Break-ups Be Like.

A part of me missed the way that he held me in his arms, while the other part of me never wanted to be touched by him, ever again.

<u>Honesty Hour.</u>

… and every time I yelled that I hated him, what I really meant was that I loved him, but I wanted to stop loving him.

I wanted him all the way out of my heart.

Holding Onto Dreams.

No matter how many times
we got it wrong

somewhere inside of me
I just always believed
that our bond was stronger than
anything
and that at some point
he and I
would eventually get it right...

I guess that's why I never strayed
and always kept myself

for him.

<u>Wisdom Words.</u>

"Listen," my aunt said. "I used to see this guy way back in the day, and he was everything to me. Literally, *everything*. But he used to make these certain remarks all the time like, 'if only you'd change so and so about yourself, and be more like this or that... you'd be perfect." I wanted to be the perfect woman for him so bad, so I changed, muted, and killed all of these parts of myself just so I could be what he wanted. Of course it worked, and I got him... but it cost me *myself*.

I say all that, to say this—there's a difference between compromising in a relationship, and selling yourself out for a relationship. Please, don't ever sell yourself out for a relationship. Wait for the man who loves, and wants you... for you."

<u>Dear God.</u>

It's almost like
the pain that you're feeling inside
is absolutely unbearable.

Isn't it?

And the tears,
no matter how much you try to fight
them,
just always seem to be stronger than
you.

Don't they?

And so you sit there,
holding your face in the palms of
your hands
and out loud you pray to God and
say—

God, please... take this pain from
me. And please let these be the last
tears that I ever cry over him.
Please.

And you know why?

Because heartbreak, is a
mutherfucker.

<u>A Craving For Balance.</u>

"You go out of your way to make sure he's good all the time," she said. "You go above and beyond to make sure he feels like a king all the time. You cater to him, and his needs, like he's never had them catered to before—and it used to feel good to do all of that, because that's your man, and you wanted to see him happy. But now you're at a point where you want to feel like royalty too. You want to feel like a queen. You want back what you've been giving out. You want to feel like you are to him, what he is to you. You want to be replenished, and I don't think that you're wrong for that at all. I think that you absolutely deserve someone who wants to see you just as happy as you want to see them... Absolutely."

Desperate Desires.

I didn't want him to understand what he had once it was too late. I didn't want him to see what I had been trying to show him the whole time after I had already walked away. I didn't fucking want him to be someone that I referred to as my past... but I guess none of that mattered.

None of it mattered because I couldn't force him to fucking get it. I couldn't force him to see me standing there giving him my all. I couldn't force him to want to stand by me, or to stand up for us, and furthermore—I didn't want to.

I wanted him to want me all on his own.

Transparent.

Right now, I can't hide it.

I try though…

I swear I do.

I put makeup on my face
I do my hair pretty
I get dressed up
and face the world with a smile…
but everyone sees it anyway.

They say it's in my eyes.

No matter how much I smile
or how put-together I look on the
outside

my eyes,
tell a story of sadness.

My eyes
tell a story of crying nights.

My eyes tell a story of
a woman
who was broken
by the same man
one too many times,
and right now…

I just can't hide it.

And one day
my eyes will tell a different story
but for now,

it just is what it is
I guess.

<u>Puppet.</u>

"You know you can let go of those strings, right?" My brother said to me. "What strings? The hell are you talking about?" I asked. "You're stressing over a guy who's dragging you along on his strings, and the only reason he's able to drag you is because you're holding onto them. Let them go so you can stop hurting yourself. He isn't worth it. Any guy who's cool with dragging you along on some strings, isn't fucking worth it."

<u>Crystal Clear.</u>

It's the part where
one day, out of nowhere,
you see what everyone else around
you has seen all along—

him for what he truly is,
and yourself for what you've become
with him.

And it makes you feel sick to your
stomach.

I think that's the part
that's always the worst,
because you're not even mad
at him anymore…

you're mad at yourself.

<u>Naked.</u>

The last thing I wanted to do was break down in front of him, but I couldn't help it. I was hurting on the inside, badly, and as much as I tried to control it… I just couldn't.

"I'm not mad at you." I said, biting my bottom lip as tears stung my cheeks. "I'm mad at myself." He inched closer to me, taking my hand in his. His touch sent jolts of both good and bad feelings throughout my body, and a rush of images through my mind—what we used to be, who he was to me, what I always imagined we were going to be together, and the reality of what we were now. I yanked my hand free and let it fall to my side.

"Stop." I whispered. "Just stop."

I felt him staring at me, aware that he didn't know what to say, and honestly, I don't think I really expected him to have anything to say. There I was, my hair as wild as a lion's mane, my eyes swollen and pouring a river of black mascara down my face, trying to keep myself standing upright… when all I wanted

to do was curl up in a little ball, and
try to scream the hurt away.

I was a fucking mess.

After about a minute of silence, I
managed to find what was left of my
voice, and spoke my truth.
"I love you; and I'm mad at myself for
believing this whole time that my
love for you would be enough to
carry us through…"

<u>Grips.</u>

In the end, it became perfectly clear that I was waiting for something that was just never going to happen with him, and it was time I got a grip on that. Shit... it was time I got a grip on myself too.

When Will It Be Me?

"It's just frustrating." I told my girl.
"And you don't want to sit there and
be on some "woe is me" tips, but
you've been so good, and given your
whole heart time after time to these
fucking guys only to end up having
them rip it up time after time, and
you just can't help but to get to a
point when you're just like yo… what
the actual fuck? When is it gonna be
my turn? When the fuck is someone
going to come into my life and give
me the same type of love, respect,
and commitment that I give out?
Fucking when?"

<u>1:47AM.</u>

I've really gotta stop giving my all
to people who don't even deserve

my half.

A little bit stronger now...

<u>Ring The Alarm.</u>

"But I love him." —that was my excuse.
That's what I would say after I was done venting to my girls. I would run through a list of all of the bad feelings that he made me feel, and all of the ways that he stressed my heart and soul every day, and at the end of it I would say, "It's just so much, and I'm so fed up... but I love him."
One day, one of my girls stopped me mid-vent and asked, "But what do you love about a man who makes you feel so bad inside? How can you tell yourself, and us, that that's love?"

And there it was...

The beginning of my wake-up call.

Note To Self.

And on a piece of paper, I
scribbled—

Any man who can fall asleep
soundly in his bed while knowing
that you're crying yourself to
sleep in yours, because of him...
is never the fucking man for you.

Then I taped that piece of paper to
my bathroom mirror, where I would
see it every morning and every
night, washed my face and went to
bed.

<u>Us VS Them.</u>

Maybe we have a hard time accepting that we can't change a man because we change for them all the time—and maybe that's our number one problem.

We change who we are for them, all the time.

<u>21 Days.</u>

"They say it takes 21 days to break a habit…" I told him, my voice cracking as I fought to hold back my tears. "And if you ever really cared about me at all, then I need you to do me a favor, and help me through this by staying away from me; because you're the habit that I need to break."

<u>Backwards.</u>

And then they'll beg you to stay

after they've spent all that time

treating you like they wanted you to
leave.

Don't Tell Me That You Love Me.

"What's my favorite color?" I asked, cutting him off in the middle of his sentence. "Huh?" He answered, confused.
"What, is my favorite color?" I repeated slowly. "It's pink," he said. I shook my head and folded my arms across my chest. "No, it's red. And I actually fucking hate the color pink." "Okay? Well close enough," he said with a shoulder shrug.
"Close enough isn't fucking good enough. What's my favorite food?" I continued. "What makes me smile the most? What touches me the most? What is my most favorite thing to do in this whole world?" He held his hand up motioning for me to stop. "Where is this all coming from, and why are you asking me all of this right now?"

As I stood there looking at him, knowing that he couldn't answer any of the questions that I'd asked him correctly… that's when it really dawned on me.

"Because," I said. "Every time I walk away from you, you beg me to come back swearing that you love me. But

how can you love someone that you
don't even fucking know?"

<u>Ain't The One.</u>

"Maybe you're not the woman for him either though," she said. "And that doesn't take away from the woman that you are. It doesn't make you inferior—it doesn't have to be a bad thing. It could simply mean that maybe you *are* too good for him, or that maybe, he's not ready for someone like you. Or maybe he wants someone who's less of a challenge—easier to manipulate and walk all over. Maybe he's got bad karma that's supposed to catch up to him, and the entire universe is working overtime to get you away from, and keep you out of that mess. It's not only them who aren't for us girl… sometimes, we ain't the ones for them either."

<u>Affirmative Thoughts.</u>

I just remember thinking—

you know what?
I owe it to myself
to be good to *myself*

for a change.

The Woman In My Mirror.

And I kept blaming him
but the truth was…

just because he called
didn't mean I had to answer
and just because he showed up at
my door

didn't mean I had to open it.

<u>Snap, Snap.</u>

I'm a firm believer of giving myself honest, raw, smack me in my face pep talks. Sometimes there is no more room for the soft toned *"don't worry, everything is gonna be okay"* shit. Sometimes, I've gotta give myself tough love—nooo, everything is NOT gonna be the fuck okay if you keep sitting in this bullshit. So that day, I said to myself "Girl, it's time to snap all the way out of it. If he really wanted to get his shit together, he would. If he really didn't want to lose you, then he'd be doing the things he's supposed to do to keep you. And if he really wanted to see you happy, then he wouldn't be making you fucking cry all the time. Period."

The 'Homewrecker' Is Him.

"So you're not going to say anything to her?!" My girl asked me, fuming. "Like you're really just going to let this random chick think that she can come through, and take your man without a fight? Really?"
I love my girl, all of my girls, but sometimes some of them don't always think before they react to shit. We've all been there, don't get me wrong, but I wasn't there anymore.

I was a calmer me... a 'think before you act', me.

"No, I'm not gonna say anything to that chick." I retorted. "For what? I don't know her, and I'm not about to beef with another chick over a dude who's put me in a position TO beef with another chick! Like? No. It doesn't matter what she thinks, what matters is what I know—and what I know is that men can't be taken from you by another woman. It ain't no hostage situation with guns to their heads. Men go where they want to go, and stay where they want to stay. It has nothing to do with her or me... it's him. He's the cheater. So what the fuck would I look like

* * *

fighting with another woman over HIM? Of course it hurts, this shit is killing me right now. But she ain't to blame, he is."

<u>La Douleur Exquise.</u>

"But what do you do when the man
that you love doesn't love you back?
I asked my mother, my eyes tired
from crying. Gently, she pushed the
wisps of hair away from my face and
said, "You love yourself enough to
let him go, accept that he's just not
the one, and have faith that God has
someone better on the way for you
babygirl."

<u>Message Sent.</u>

Here's the thing:

Every day I left my house, random strangers stopped me only to look at me in my eyes and tell me that I was beautiful. I would smile and thank them, of course, but they weren't the ones I wanted to hear that from—I wanted to hear it from you.

At the end of every conversation that I'd have with a man, I'd be told how refreshing my mind was and how impressed they were with the natural way that I carried myself. I was flattered and grateful, of course, but in the back of my mind I couldn't help but wish that you would acknowledge those very things about me too.

Every single day someone new would tell me how lucky the man in my life was to have me, and that they hoped he truly understood what he had by his side… and I remember being ashamed of myself. Ashamed, because there I was standing loyal by the side of a man who couldn't even do the smallest of things to show that he appreciated the woman that I was—and this isn't

me saying all of this to shit on you,
or put all of the blame on you by the
way—this is just me being honest
with you, and with myself at the
same time.

Driving On One Way Roads.

Knowing how to please a man
was never my problem.
My problem,
was finding a man
who knew how to please me back.

I Don't Need You.

"You know what?" I wrote in the text.
"I did need you. So what? I don't
even care how that makes me look,
or sound—we're humans, and we all
need someone at some point or
another, and I needed you.
I needed you to be the man that you
said you were going to be for me—
supportive, caring, and fucking
reliable. I needed you to be my
teammate. That's what you
promised to be, remember?
So now when I say that I *don't* need
you, it's not because I'm throwing
the independent woman "I don't
need no man" card in the air. No.
It's that I don't need a man who
cannot keep his fucking word."

<u>Reminders.</u>

And when I yelled,

"I AM A GOOD FUCKING WOMAN"
through my tears,

it wasn't because I was trying to
convince him of it…

It was because I had to fucking
remind *myself*.

<u>Time.</u>

Some days I blame him, other days
I blame myself.
Some days I chalk it up to us being
two people who simply didn't work
out.
Some days I can't stand the thought
of him, other days, he's all I want to
think of.
Some days I ask God to hurry up
and take him out of my heart… help
me to fall out of love.
And maybe it'll be like that for a
while—in and out of my emotions,
back and forth in my mind.
And maybe I need to stop beating
myself up because of it, I mean shit,
I should know better…

the healing process takes time.

<u>Metanoia.</u>

I used to fight so hard,
and with everything in me,
to hold on to you…

to hold on to us.

Now I'm fighting with everything in
me to let go of you,
and to let go…

of us.

<u>Savage, Unapologetically.</u>

"I miss you," was the first text from him. I was prepared to ignore it, but then a second one came through right after it that said, "I just wanna come back to you." — and that one, I just couldn't ignore.
I laughed out loud to myself—you know the angry/sarcastic/insulted type of laughs? And then I wrote back, "No no, you chose to be with her, remember? You wanted to go 'dabble in new waters' so now stay there... and fucking drown."

Checkmate.

"I want to be your man," he said.
"No you don't," I replied. "You just
want to make sure that you have me
all to yourself—a peace of mind
knowing that you've got a 'good
woman' tucked away at home and
representing you well when she's
out in public, while you're out there
doing whatever and whoever it is
that you want. Keep it real… you
don't really want to be my man; you
just want me to be your woman."

Self-Worth

Maybe I don't want to be
someone else's woman
right now.

Maybe, right now…

I want to be my own woman.

Declaration.

My purpose in life
isn't to sit around

waiting, or begging,
for *any* man
to finally come to his senses

and treat me right.

<u>Once Upon A Time.</u>

I was your favorite doll, wasn't I?

I sat beautifully contained in a box
on the shelf of a house that only you
had the keys to.

My hair, pretty and always on point.
My face, smooth and youthful.
My lips, perfectly painted with the
right amount of Crimson.
My skin, an even color of caramel.
My body, soft and comforting like
Egyptian Cotton.
My pussy, tight and reserved only...
for you.

I sat beautifully contained in a box
on the shelf of house that only you
had the keys to, and only came to
life when you decided that you
wanted to pick me up and play with
me.

Yes, I was your favorite doll...

wasn't I?

Audacity At Its Finest.

He wanted all of me
in exchange for parts of him,
and then called me "complicated"
when I said…

no.

<u>Cowardly Behavior.</u>

Yep, he was angry.
He called me a few names, and told
anyone who would listen that I
turned out to be 'this and that'.
But funny enough, he always
conveniently forgot to mention all of
the real life shit that he did to me,
how long I took the shit for, and how
many excuses I made for all of the
shit before I turned around and
became the 'this and that'.
But, it's okay. It's truly all good.
Because I understand now, that he's
a coward...

and that's just the type of shit that
cowards do.

<u>Epiphany.</u>

"I was praying for the wrong thing," I told my girl. "How do you figure?" She asked. "I spent all of those months in bed at night with my eyes closed, praying to unlove him, when really… I should have been praying for the strength to love myself more."

Truth Serum.

"The sad thing about it all," she said, "is that you've spent a lot of time feeling like you weren't good enough, all because you were in the hands of men who weren't man enough."

Your Turn.

"I'm gonna be honest with you," she said. "Even though I know this isn't what you wanna hear right now, I'ma say it anyway 'cause you're my girl—you need to let someone new into your life. He doesn't have to be a potential 'boyfriend' or a 'lover', but you need to be refreshed. You need to give someone else a shot at making you smile, making you laugh—even just texting you a 'good morning' or a 'how's your day?' or a 'good night'. You need to let someone new court you for a while. You know why? Because little things like that are what's gonna show you that life has to go on for you too, and not just for the guy who left you behind.

I know you're hurting, and I know this heartbreak shit isn't easy, but keeping yourself closed off isn't what's going to make it any better. The guy who broke your heart is out there living, thinking about himself. It's your turn now. It's your turn to live, and for fucking once, start thinking about yourself too."

<u>Salt Water.</u>

"You've got a whole lot more to offer
this world, than merely tears of
sadness. Trust me," she said,
"Dig deeper."

<u>Soldiers.</u>

Being brave is picking yourself up off
of the floor even though your heart is
still screaming out in pain from
inside of you, wiping your tears, and
continuing on with the faith that one
day you're gonna be okay again.

I don't give a shit what anyone
says…

to me, that's bravery at its finest.

<u>The Weakest Arms.</u>

"You could have left me where I was you know," I told him. "I didn't need to be lifted up by another pair of arms that would only drop me, yet again. You could have left me right where I was, and eventually, I would have lifted my damn self up."

<u>A Good Woman.</u>

It was time. I'd had enough.
My mind was tired, my heart was
tired, and it may sound stupid to
some, but, I felt like I was at rock
bottom. So while I was down there,
alone with myself, I thought about
what I needed…

and it hit me.

I had to learn how to be a good
woman to myself, first.

<u>Sulit.</u>

It was important for me, as a woman,
to learn how to build a life of my
own—separate from any man—so
that if shit ever hit the fan, I'd still
have my own identity…

I'd still have my own life.

<u>Organic Over Forced.</u>

I don't want anything from you

that you don't want to give me

on your own.

<u>Treasure Chest.</u>

He was right.
I was too loving
too touchy-feely
too deep
too sensitive
too passionate
too caring
too romantic
too involved…

too much.

I was, and still am,
all of those things.

And he didn't, and still doesn't,

deserve a woman like me.

Karma

I didn't wish him all the best,
because that would be a lie, but I
didn't wish him all the worst either. I
simply wished him whatever it was
he deserved.
Now, whether he deserved good
things or bad things, was none of my
business—that was between him
and karma.

Just Fine.

"I think that I'm a little afraid." I told my girl as we walked. "Of?" She asked. I shrugged my shoulders. "I've given so much to the wrong men, and like the good stuff. You know? The loyalty, the catering, the nurturing, the efforts, the love—the shit that you're supposed to give in a relationship—and I guess I'm a little afraid that when the right man does come along, I'm going to be reluctant to give that stuff again, and I'm gonna fuck up a good thing because of it." She thought for a second and then turned to me, "But you know what? The right guy is going to understand where you're coming from, and he's going to have all of the patience in the world for you. He'll take his time, and go at your pace. He'll work with you, instead of against you. He'll come into your life and make things easier for you, instead of harder... because that's what the right guys do B. Don't worry," She threw her arm around my shoulder. "You're gonna be just fine."

These Praying Hands Of Mine

I laid in my bed staring up at the
ceiling, and wondered why I felt bad
for him… why I felt… sad for him.
I mean, he was the one who broke
me after all, and while I could feel all
of my broken pieces floating around
inside of me, and should have been
angry at him… for some reason, I
just wasn't.
Maybe somewhere far in the back of
my mind I knew that he didn't do it
on purpose.
Maybe somewhere deep in the core
of my heart I knew that he was a
good guy who happened to have
made a mistake.
Or maybe, part of me knew that
breaking me, broke him too.
I don't know.
But whatever it was it kept me
awake that night, and instead of
being angry at him, I felt bad and
sad for him, and ended up praying
and asking God to help heal him too.

Hennessy And A Cellphone.

Still have all these pictures of you in
my phone
that I should probably delete
text message threads that go all the
way back to last year
with proof of the arguments we
tended to constantly repeat.
But it wasn't all bad, there's a lot of
good in those message threads too.
Receipts of how I always had your
back, and how in return, you always
had mine too.
It's sad the way shit ended,
I always thought our love could
withstand anything
I hate the way shit ended,
God knows you were my everything.
All of these reminders of you in my
phone
that I should probably delete
but damn it...
I just can't bring myself to do that
yet.

Better Over Bitter.

I went through my stretch of
bitterness after him, yes, but there
came a point when I had to snap out
of it, because staying bitter would
have made him the winner.
You understand what I'm saying?

Staying bitter wouldn't have done
me any good, or attracted anything
good into my life either.
Staying bitter would have only sent
all good things, and people, running
in the opposite direction—and I
didn't want that.

He had already controlled too much
of me while we were together... and
staying bitter meant that he'd get to
control the rest of my life, without
him even having to be in it.

<u>Q&A.</u>

He asked me if he ever crossed my mind, and so, I told him the truth:

"Yes. Whenever I see another woman spilling tears uncontrollably, while clutching her chest because her heart hurts so bad from finding out that the man she loves has betrayed, embarrassed, and took advantage of her. When I can see that woman is torn in two, and tortured between wanting to believe that the promises he's feeding her aren't empty, and everyone around her—including her own gut—is screaming to walk away. That's when you cross my mind… because I was once that woman too, all thanks to you."

<u>Reflections Of A Growing Woman.</u>

We get into these relationships with men while we're in our young 20's, and as we grow and look back on those relationships, we're able to see that a lot of the mistakes we made were because we didn't know better yet. We hadn't figured things out for ourselves yet. We didn't even really know ourselves yet… and it makes me think—maybe a lot of the mistakes that men made with us, was because they didn't really know themselves back then either…

Holding myself accountable
X
Seeing things a bit clearer...

<u>Hourglasses.</u>

I fucked up.
And where I fucked up is probably
where a lot of us fuck up—I waited.
I waited for him to come around.
I waited to see if things would get
better. I waited to see if he would
become the man that I imagined him
becoming.
All of this fucking waiting, and before
I knew it, a bunch of years had
passed me by and I was still doing
the same old shit…

waiting.

<u>Spilled Words.</u>

"Do you miss me?" He asked. "Like crazy," I admitted. "So come home." He said.
Hearing those words made my heart skip, and normally—if we were to look back into our history—I would have gone. My mind would yell 'don't you dare' but my heart would yell louder 'he's your everything' and I would have listened to my heart.
But this time... was different.

My ear to the phone, I closed my eyes, and let my mind play a series of flashbacks of all of the times that I did run back, only to end up running away again, with a face full of tears. I couldn't keep doing this to myself. If insanity was doing the same thing over and over again, expecting different results, well... I was driving myself insane.

It took everything in me to say the words that I said out loud, but, they had to be said, and I had to mean them. It was time I saved myself. "I love you, and I miss you," I told him. "But you can't be my home anymore."

Truth Owner

Did he really break my heart over
and over again?
Or was I the one who kept breaking
my own heart by settling for a
relationship that I knew deep down,
didn't sit right with me, hoping over
and over again that it would
magically change on its own?
I was, after all, responsible for
myself—wasn't I?
I had choices in this world just like
everyone else—didn't I?
It was up to me to teach people how
to treat me—wasn't it?

Fuck... I fucked up.

Somewhere along the line I
misplaced my self-worth, and
blamed it on him. Somewhere along
the line I started lying to myself, and
blamed it on him. Somewhere along
the line I started hating myself for
staying loyal to a relationship that
was killing me on the inside, and
instead of taking accountability for
what I was doing to myself...
I blamed it all, on him.

Fuck... I fucked up.

Wiping Steam Off Of The Mirrors.

See, we're only as good as the company we keep—which, by the way—includes the men that we sleep with, and entertain as well.

Freedom.

It's crazy because, I went through
this period where my motivation to
do better came only from wanting
him to bump into me randomly one
day, see me at my best, and get
angry at himself for ever letting me
go, or doing me wrong.
But as the days and weeks passed, I
let go of all those thoughts. I didn't
give a shit anymore about being at
my best just to make him angry...
I gave a shit about being at my best,
to make *myself happy*.

<u>Humble Facts.</u>

My last relationship taught me
that I needed to step my self-worth
game up.

<u>Happily In Love.</u>

He asked what he could do to make things right between him and I, and I said —

"There will never be another you and I again. That's over, and I'm not going back to you, ever; there's just too much damage in our history. But, if you're really looking to make some type of truce with me, then just don't ever treat another woman that comes into your life the way you did me—because no woman deserves that, and I don't care who she is. I'd rather see a woman who is happily in love with you, than one who is praying to unlove you the way that I once was."

A New Me.

I'm willing to compromise when it comes to many things—but not love man. Not love.
I've done that too many times and it has taught me exactly what I want from what I don't want.
And listen… it's not like the type of love I want is from a fairytale… no.
The love I want is a very real thing—it's out there, and it has nothing to do with posting fucking pictures or dropping everything to immediately answer text messages that aren't even urgent—that shit is high school to me.

What I want in love, is respect, even when an argument arises. I never want to cry my eyes out till I'm sick because of an argument, ever again.
I want a love that has commitment, tenderness, laughter, playfulness, passion, morals, and above all else, I want a love that is always felt.
I never want to have to question whether or not that man that I'm giving all of myself to really loves me, ever again. And never again will I *ever* entertain a man who tells me that I'm asking for too much.

I know what I want.

What I want exists.

And if one man doesn't want to give
it me, then I won't break my head
over it—he's simply not for me.

<u>Owning My Truth.</u>

"Can we please, just try again?" He begged. "No," I answered, completely sure of myself. "This is crazy," he said. "Why are you doing this? When you love someone, you don't just give up on them, you keep trying. Remember?"

Me? Keep trying? Was he serious?

"See, that's your problem right there," I told him. "You think that the definition of love is staying by someone's side no matter how poorly they treat you, and take advantage of you..." I stopped for a second, thinking about what I had just said—and it hit me. "And you know what? Maybe that was my problem all along too... because I stayed through all of this shit and called it love, over and over again. So actually, I'm gonna go ahead and apologize for teaching you how to love me wrong, and then blaming you for following through."

<u>Amour Propre.</u>

I knew that I had reached
an ultimate level of self-respect,
when I stopped begging that man
to love me properly.

<u>Bitter Sweet.</u>

"Hold on," he says, as he reaches across the table to smooth a strand of hair away from my face. I smile as I blush and lower my eyes. "Thank you," I say to him.

I'm shy. This is new. I'm not used to this, so I keep my eyes lowered, not knowing what else to say.
Again, he reaches back across the table, this time, he gently places the tip of his finger under my chin. Slowly, I look up at him to find that his eyes are deadlocked on mine. More blushing. Fuck. I know my entire face is probably bright crimson.

He smiles at me. A warm smile. A genuine smile.
"I don't think you even know just how incredibly beautiful you truly are, as a whole," he says.
Again, I lower my eyes, but this time it's because they're filled with water.

It's sad, you know? It's sad when you're so used to being with someone who neglected you from the gentle words and the gentle touches that you've needed and

craved for so long, that when it
finally happens...
when someone finally touches you
and speaks to you like that...

it's almost like you don't even
believe them.

<u>Saving You From Me.</u>

"I need you to walk on by me." I said to him. "What?" He asked. "Why would you say that? I want to be right here with you. What do you mean walk on by you?"

He was confused, and rightfully so. I shook my head. "Listen," I said. "I know what it's like to be lied to, so I don't wanna do that to you. I know what it's like to be strung along, too, and I don't wanna do that to you either. The truth is, I'm not in the state to have anyone try to get close to me right now. I have some left over broken pieces inside of me that I need to deal with, on my own.

You're a good man. A really, really good man. And I can tell that all you want to do is make my life a little easier… a little brighter… a little safer. But, I'd rather let a good man like you walk on by, than stay beside me while I know that I may accidentally cut you with my broken pieces. I know I probably sound crazy to you right now, but, I'm only doing for you what I wish the person before you would have done for me.

● ● ●

So please… let me save you from
me. Just let me do the right thing by
telling you to walk on by me."

<u>Him.</u>

It takes a certain type of man to be able to get it.
To understand that a woman who's used to being let down repetitively, and starved of the simplest things in a relationship—like peace, tenderness, common respect, and is used to always having to fight to be heard—doesn't know what a "happy" relationship feels like. So it takes a certain type of man to want her to know that feeling, and have the patience to simply walk her through it as she gets used to a new normal. A loving normal. A breathe easy normal. A stress free normal.
A genuinely happy normal.
And when I saw the way he refused to give up on me... that's when I knew, he was that man.

<u>Protective Walls.</u>

"What scares you?" He asked me. We were sitting outside, shoulder to shoulder, and I looked up into the night sky as I thought about his question for a second. "Honestly," I started. "I think that I'm scared of letting a man be there for me, or even do stuff for me. And it's weird, because I do want a man to be there and to do stuff for me—the normal stuff like courting me, or helping me out here and there if I need it, or just all of the things that a man is supposed to want to do for a woman naturally. But the last time I let a man do things for me, he made sure to throw them all right back in my face. And I guess that I'm just scared of giving someone else the opportunity to do that again.

<u>Magnificent Mess.</u>

"You're a mess," he said. "I know I
am," I responded. "But there's
magnificence in the mess that you
are," he continued. "Were you aware
of that?" I smiled and blushed a little,
as I looked down, and then back up
at him. "I'm starting to be."

<u>Kilig.</u>

"Getting to know someone new is this weird mix between exciting, and scary," I told my girl. "It's like, yes, I fucking looove the butterflies that I've got flying around in my tummy, they feel so damn good. But at the same time, I'm also like… are you going to take me to the point of falling in love with you, only to turn into a fucking monster once I've fallen? Because I swear to God that I can't deal with another fucking heartbreak man. I just *cannot*."

The Key.

… and when he asked what it was that he could give to me, that I'd never had before, my answer was simple. "Consistency," I said. "If you want to give me something that every other man has yet to give me, then don't give me mixed signals and emotions that leave me wondering. I'm tired of wondering. I don't want to play guessing games. If you're gonna be here with me, then be here. If you ever feel the need to leave, then stay gone. All I want from someone at this point, is consistency."

<u>No Settling.</u>

I don't want to be someone's "girl".
I've already had that title a couple of
times before and it doesn't mean shit
to me anymore, so this time around,
if I'm going to be someone's
anything, then I've gotta be their
whole heart… and nothing less.

<u>Familiar Eyes.</u>

"So who is this new guy?" He pressed. "No one you know, and none of your business," I told him. "Is it serious?" He continued. "It's serious enough," I answered, getting annoyed. He stared at me silently.

"What?" I asked. "Why are you asking me these things? Matter of fact, why do you even care? You left me, remember? So why do you care who I'm with now, or whether or not it's serious? I'm happy. I'm at peace, and he loves me with his whole heart. I don't wander into your life, disturbing you, so if you could kindly not wander into mine and disturb me, that would be really great." Again, he stayed silent as he stared at me. "Jesus Christ!" I yelled. "What?! What do you want from me?"

"Just one more question, and then I'll leave you alone," he said. "How do you know that he loves you already?"

I looked at my ex, and shook my head. "Because the way he looks at me when he thinks I'm not looking, is the way that I used to look at you..."

The Light Inside Of The
Tunnel...

Le Coeur Solide.

This heart of mine
survived every hand
that held it
with the intent
to kill it.

<u>Her.</u>

I'm that girl who'll thug it out. Give chances. Have patience, make room for growth, and try again. But once I've reached my limit, I'll leave without saying a word… and you'll never hear from me again.

Believe that.

<u>If Only.</u>

He told me that he wished he had loved me better back then.

Shit…

I wish I had loved myself better back then too.

Embracing The Journey.

And then there are women like me—
no longer afraid to show people that
we're humans, and that we cry, hurt,
scream, and feel weak sometimes—
just like everyone else. We've
stopped apologizing for not being
perfect a long time ago, because
we've learned that perfect isn't a real
thing. We've also learned that
strength isn't about being
bulletproof, but instead, about the
will to survive the bullets, and being
able to forgive those who have fired
them at us. Not for their peace of
mind, but for our own.
Women like me don't pretend
anymore to have it all together 24/7.
We're growing through life one day
at a time, and doing the best that we
can...

one day at a time.

<u>Rhapsodic.</u>

Yes I am an extremely sensitive and emotional person. I don't only feel my emotions very deeply, but I feel everyone else's too.
Throughout the years I've been brainwashed into believing that this is my "problem", but I've realized that actually no, this is not my problem…
This is my *gift.*
My problem, was staying around people who were unable to properly value, and appreciate that gift.

Trust Issues.

One of the many important things that I've learned along the way, is that often, the best advice we can ever seek out is from within. Our intuition really does know best. We always feel whether what we are doing is right or wrong for us, and whether we are involved with the right or wrong people. We are forever asking others what we should do when it comes to matters of the heart, when really, deep down we already know—it's *our* heart. The problem is that we constantly ignore ourselves while we search for answers everywhere else, and then we have the nerve to ask others to trust us. But, how dare we?

How dare we ask to be trusted when we spend so much time not trusting ourselves.

<u>It Is What It Is.</u>

Once a year, without fail, he finds a
way to send me a message saying
that he's still yet to find anyone quite
like me.
And once a year, without fail, I leave
his message unanswered, but think
to myself…

and you never will, again.

The Ox.

If you're anything like me, then
you're hard as fuck on yourself.
You often forgive others for their
mistakes easily, but when it comes
to your own, you'll hold grudges
against yourself forever—but you're
working on that part now.

You're passionate, ambitious,
determined, and fighting hard to get
something that you want isn't
something that you're scared of—it
actually isn't something new.
You've learned to be hella tough on
the outside, but on the inside, man...
you're super sensitive with a heart
that is way bigger than you. You
have a smart ass mouth (a gift and a
curse) but it's really only used as a
defense mechanism towards those
who think they can walk all over you.

You consider your few friends as
family, and when it comes to men,
all you want is someone who will go
as hard for you as you'll go for
them... because if you're anything
like me, then going hard in life is just
what you do, and slowly, you're
starting to realize that maybe that's
not such a bad thing after all.

<u>Dear Younger Self.</u>

What would I go back and tell my younger self if I could?
Fuck. So much.
But I guess I would start with telling her to speak up for herself when she's feeling uncomfortable in a situation, and to hold her middle finger in the air towards whoever doesn't like it.
To not enter any relationships with boys until she builds a solid bond with herself first. To spend more time with her girls—having *fun* being carefree and young—rather than rushing to grow up so quickly.
That her wild and messy curls are beautiful just the way they are, and if the only way that she's gonna "fit in" is to straighten them all the time, then she doesn't fucking need to fit it anywhere.
And if I had to leave her with one last thing, I would tell her that her big heart is not a gift and curse, but instead, a gift and a blessing—but to just be really careful who she gives it to; because not everyone she'll meet will know how to take care of it the way it will need to be taken care of.

Then And Now.

I used to fight, scream, beg, and
hold on as tightly as I could—that's
what I used to do.
But I'm learning as I go along in life
how to happily, and gracefully, let go
of anyone who doesn't want to be
kept by me. I shouldn't have to fight
for a man to appreciate me.
I shouldn't have to scream for a man
to stop hurting me. And I shouldn't
have to beg for any man to love
me—in fact—I shouldn't ever *want* a
love that I have to beg for.
I'm a little smarter now.
I'm a little stronger now.
I've been treating myself better
lately.
I've been cherishing myself more
lately.

My heart is the same, but my mind
works a little differently now—and I
like it. I love it.

My favorite thing to hear is people
telling me that I've changed, cause
damn it…
it was about time that I did.

Single And Serene.

It's okay to be the single girl who's picky as fuck when it comes to men, you know? It's okay to be the single girl who knows what she wants, deserves, and won't bend for anyone who isn't willing to give her both—can't let anyone try to make you feel bad for that. You're allowed to stand firmly in your worth once you've figured it out. You're allowed to be the single girl who'd rather be single and joyous, than committed to the wrong person and miserable as all fuck.

F.Y.I

See, when we're too soft, you walk
all over us. But when we're too
rough, you call us "bitches."
If we're too quiet, you tell us to
speak up and speak our minds.
But if we're too loud and speak up
too often, you call us "nags".
When we're reserved you tell us to
loosen up a bit, but when we do, you
call us "sluts".
If we're "sluts" you shame the shit
out of us, but if we're good girls, you
cheat on us with the very "sluts" you
just shamed.
You tell us that you need a woman
with a good head on her shoulders,
but then choose the one with the
fattest ass, fuck her raw, and get her
pregnant.
You tell us you want a strong woman
who knows who she is and loves
herself, but then you get her, and
break her down until her insides are
torn to shreds, then move onto the
next, leaving her alone with her pain.
And you wonder why we women
band together so often to get on our
"*women empowerment shit*" as you
like to call it, because yes, if we
don't help each other out... who will?
Clearly, not men like fucking you.

The Light Inside Of The Tunnel.

I know where my power is now—it's
in my truths.
It's admitting what I've been through,
but also owning what I've put myself
through. It's accepting that I can't
ever undo the past, but knowing that
I needed it to learn things about
myself, and my surroundings, that
nothing or no one else could ever
teach me.
I know where my power is now...

my power, is in my truths.

SPILLED WORDS

THE CRIMSON KISS QUOTE COLLECTION

Cici. B